WORKBOOK

LEVEL B

A Hen in a Fox's Den

by Donald Rasmussen and Lynn Goldberg

Columbus, Ohio

*A Division of The **McGraw·Hill** Companies*

Copyright © 2000 by SRA/McGraw-Hill. All rights reserved. Except as permitted under the United States Copyright Act, no part of this publication may be reproduced or distributed in any form or by any means, or stored in a database or retrieval system, without prior written permission from the publisher.

Printed in the United States of America.

Send all inquiries to:
SRA/McGraw-Hill
250 Old Wilson Bridge Road, Suite 310
Worthington, OH 43085

ISBN 0-02-6840065

1 2 3 4 5 6 7 8 9 0 DBH 05 04 03 02 01 00 99

_a_	_i_	_e_	_o_	_u_
bat	bit	bet		but
cat			cot	cut
			dot	
		get	got	
hat	hit		hot	hut
		jet	jot	jut
	kit			
	lit	let	lot	
mat		met		
Nat		net	not	nut
pat	pit	pet	pot	
rat			rot	rut
sat	sit	set		
		wet		
		yet		

SECTION 1 LETTER-SOUND CONTENT (pp. 1–15)
Review: Consonant letters from Level A
    Medial vowels a, i
New: CVC spelling pattern —t (nut)
    Medial vowels e, o, u
    Initial consonants y as in yet and g as in got

hat

☐ cat

☐ cot

☐ **Dot**

☐ pot

1

2

3

4

5

PURPOSES OF THIS PAGE
1. to promote automatic word recognition

☐ jet

☐ net

☐ pet

☐ hut

☐ nut

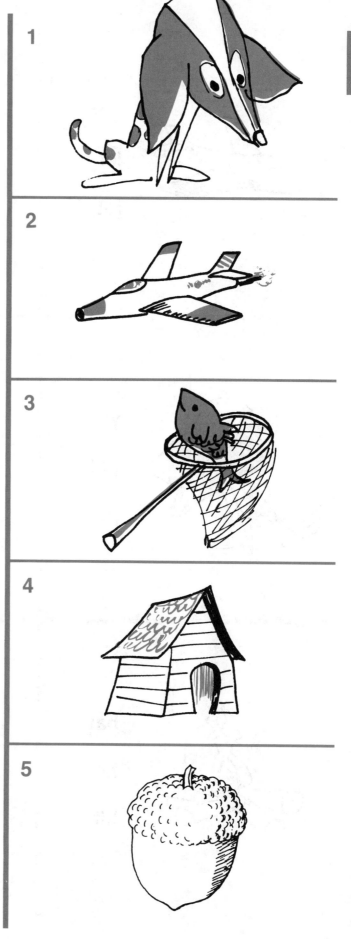

1

PURPOSES OF THIS PAGE
1. to promote automatic word recognition
2. to promote word comprehension through picture associations

1

get

(jet)

jot

pot

got

dot

yet

pot

pet

hut

not

nut

hat

hot

hit

hit

hut

hat

PURPOSES OF THIS PAGE
1. to promote automatic word recognition
2. to contrast words of similar spelling or configuration
3. to promote word comprehension through picture associations

wet

yet

met

dot

cot

cat

met

not

net

cut

cot

cat

dot

pot

pat

met

net

mat

1. to promote automatic word recognition
2. to contrast words of similar spelling or configuration
3. to promote word comprehension through picture associations

1

 A pot tips.

 A cot tips.

 The pets met.

 The pigs met.

 Dan cuts.

 Dot cuts.

○ **A pet is wet.**

○ **A net is wet.**

PURPOSES OF THIS PAGE
1. to promote automatic word recognition within sentences
2. to promote sentence comprehension through picture associations

1

2

3

4

PURPOSES OF THIS PAGE
1. to promote automatic word recognition within sentences
2. to reinforce sentence comprehension through picture associations
3. to give practice in picture interpretation

3   **The van got into a rut.**

     The pets got wet.

     The pot is hot.

     The pet is in the net.

1

The pig began to get
- yet.
- (wet.)
- set.

The cat met a big
- pot.
- pit.
- pet.

The cab is in a bad
- hut.
- nut.
- rut.

The pets sat in a
- pat.
- pit.
- pot.

PURPOSES OF THIS PAGE
1. to promote automatic word recognition within sentences
2. to contrast words of similar spelling or configuration
3. to promote sentence comprehension through picture associations

⊗ Tim said, "The pet has a lot of nuts."

◯ Jim said, "The pet has a lot of nets."

◯ "Rags did not get it yet," said Al.

◯ "I let Rags get the net," said Al.

◯ "Tim's pet is in the pot," said Dot.

◯ "Dan's pot is in the pit," said Dot.

◯ "I did not let Dot into the hut," said Rags.

◯ "I did not let Kit into the hut," said Rags.

PURPOSES OF THIS PAGE
1. to promote automatic word recognition within sentences
2. to give practice in reading sentences containing quotations
3. to promote sentence comprehension through picture associations

1

1

2

3

4

☐ "I got it in a net," said Kim,
"but I got wet."

☐ "It is hot," said Tim,
"but the cot is not hot yet."

☐ "The bad pet hid," said Tim,
"but I can get him."

☐ "I can pet it," said Pam,
"and I can get it wet."

PURPOSES OF THIS PAGE
1. to promote automatic word recognition within sentences
2. to give practice in reading sentences containing quotations
3. to promote sentence comprehension through picture associations
4. to give practice in picture interpretation

Dot can get into the

net.

jet.

pet.

Al met Peg at the

hut.

hat.

hit.

Wag let Kit into his

pot.

pet.

pit.

Dot cuts the big

net.

not.

nut.

PURPOSES OF THIS PAGE
1. to promote automatic word recognition within sentences
2. to contrast words of similar spelling or configuration
3. to promote sentence comprehension through picture associations

Can it?

○ Can a net rip?

○ Can a nut fit in a net?

○ Can a pet get hot?

○ Can a pot get wet?

○ Can a dot pet a pot?

○ Can Dot cut a nut?

○ Can a hut sit in a pot?

○ Can a pet get a lot of nuts?

PURPOSES OF THIS PAGE
1. to promote automatic word recognition within sentences that are questions
2. to promote sentence comprehension and interpretation
3. to give practice in detecting absurdities
4. to encourage creative and imaginative responses for discussion

It can get hot.

It can get wet.

It is as big as a hat.

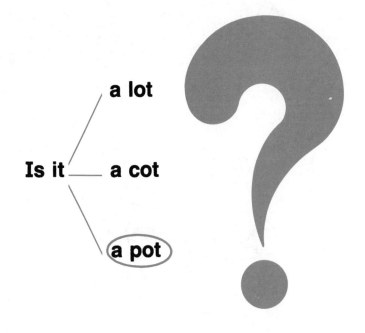

Is it — a lot
Is it — a cot
Is it — (a pot)

It can sit in a hut.

It can get a lot of nuts.

It can get big and fat.

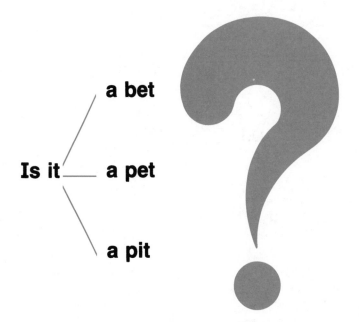

Is it — a bet
Is it — a pet
Is it — a pit

PURPOSES OF THIS PAGE
1. to promote automatic word recognition within sentences
2. to contrast phrases containing words of similar spelling or configuration
3. to promote sentence and paragraph comprehension
4. to give practice in reasoning logically and drawing conclusions

Is it in the hut?

⊗ **a bag**   ◯ **a dot**

◯ **a pot**   ◯ **a rut**

◯ **a pit**   ◯ **a jet**

◯ **a nut**   ◯ **a net**

◯ **a cot**   ◯ **a pet**

PURPOSES OF THIS PAGE
1. to promote automatic word recognition within phrases
2. to promote phrase comprehension through picture associations
3. to give practice in picture interpretation

It can get a rip in it.

A pet can get in it.

It is as big as a pot.

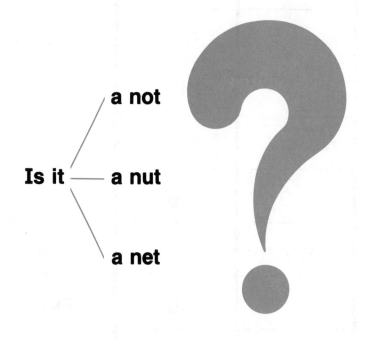

Is it ── a not

Is it ── a nut

Is it ── a net

A van can get into it.

A cab can get into it.

Wag and Kit can sit in it.

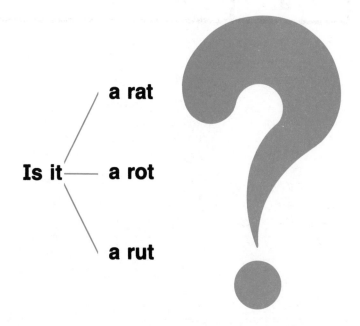

Is it ── a rat

Is it ── a rot

Is it ── a rut

PURPOSES OF THIS PAGE
1. to promote automatic word recognition within sentences
2. to contrast phrases containing words of similar spelling or configuration
3. to promote sentence and paragraph comprehension
4. to give practice in reasoning logically and drawing conclusions

__ a __	__ i __	__ e __	__ o __	__ u __
bag	big	beg		bug
	dig		dog	dug
	fig		fog	
hag			hog	hug
	jig		jog	jug
lag		leg	log	lug
	pig	peg		
rag				rug
tag				tug
wag	wig			

2

SECTION 2 LETTER-SOUND CONTENT (pp. 16–30)
Review: Consonant letters
Medial vowel letters *a, i, e, o, u*
New: CVC spelling pattern —*g (beg)*

☐ **dog**

☐ **hog**

☐ **log**

☐ **jug**

☐ **rug**

1

2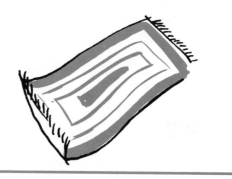

3

4

5

2

PURPOSES OF THIS PAGE
1. to promote automatic word recognition
2. to promote word comprehension through picture associations

2

☐ **leg**

☐ **Peg**

☐ **beg**

☐ **bug**

☐ **dug**

1

2

3

4

5

PURPOSES OF THIS PAGE
1. to promote automatic word recognition
2. to promote word comprehension through picture associations

 a big dog

◯ **a big log**

 ◯ **a fat bug**

◯ **a fat bag**

◯ **a big map**

◯ **a hot mug**

◯ **a pet pig**

◯ **a wet fog**

◯ **a wet rut**

◯ **a wet rug**

◯ **a sad dog**

◯ **a mad hog**

2

PURPOSES OF THIS PAGE
1. to promote automatic word recognition within phrases
2. to contrast phrases containing words of similar spelling or configuration
3. to promote phrase comprehension through picture associations

19

○ **a dog in the fog**

○ **a hog in the hut**

○ **jets in the fog**

○ **pets and a rug**

○ **a hog in a jug**

○ **a bug in a rug**

○ **a bug and a nut**

○ **a jug and a mug**

○ **a pet in the fog**

○ **a dog in the log**

○ **a dog and a log**

○ **a bug and a leg**

PURPOSES OF THIS PAGE
1. to promote automatic word recognition within phrases
2. to contrast phrases containing words of similar spelling or configuration
3. to promote phrase comprehension through picture associations

○ Jim has a bad leg.

○ Jim sat to cut logs.

○ Meg can hug the pets.

○ Meg can lug the pots.

○ A fat bug bit Wag's leg.

○ A big dog dug a pit.

○ The hog sits.

○ The dog naps.

PURPOSES OF THIS PAGE
1. to promote automatic word recognition within sentences
2. to promote sentence comprehension through picture associations

1

2

3

4

☐ Meg lugs a big bag.

☐ Wag begs to get his pan.

☐ Jim hugs his pet in his lap.

☐ Kit dug a pit and ran.

PURPOSES OF THIS PAGE
1. to promote automatic word recognition within sentences
2. to reinforce sentence comprehension through picture associations
3. to give practice in picture interpretation

Kim can hit it. It is a

pot.

peg.

pet.

2

It is in a hut. It is a

rut.

rug.

rat.

The man can cut it. It is a

log.

fog.

leg.

Dot has a pal. It is

Peg.

a pet.

a pot.

PURPOSES OF THIS PAGE
1. to promote automatic word recognition within sentences
2. to contrast words of similar spelling or configuration
3. to promote sentence comprehension through picture associations

○ Kim said to Wag, "Sit and beg."

○ Tim said to Rags, "Sit and dig."

○ "The dog dug in the rug," said Dad.

○ "I dug a pit in the fog," said the hog.

○ "I can tug at the rug," said the hog.

○ "I can get into the jug," said the bug.

○ Jim said, "I can hug the dog."

○ The dog said, "I can tug at the rug."

24

PURPOSES OF THIS PAGE
1. to promote automatic word recognition within sentences
2. to give practice in reading sentences containing quotations
3. to promote sentence comprehension through picture associations

2

PURPOSES OF THIS PAGE
1. to promote automatic word recognition within sentences
2. to give practice in reading sentences containing quotations
3. to promote sentence comprehension through picture associations
4. to give practice in picture interpretation

☐ Dad said, "It is big. Peg can hug it, but Peg cannot lug it."

☐ Dad said, "It's a bad bug. It bit the dog's leg."

☐ The cat said, "I can lug Kit. I can get Kit to the rug."

☐ The dog said, "I can tag Kit. Kit's leg is in the rug."

Tim is not sad. Tim hugs his

dog.

hog.

Dad.

Peg ran and got a

mug.

peg.

pin.

Dot and Meg can tug at a

log.

bug.

leg.

Tim's pet began to tug at his

let.

leg.

log.

PURPOSES OF THIS PAGE
1. to promote automatic word recognition within sentences
2. to contrast words of similar spelling or configuration
3. to promote sentence comprehension through picture associations

Can it?

◯ **Can a rug fit in a hut?**

◯ **Can a jug get hot and wet?**

◯ **Can a bug hug a leg?**

◯ **Can a bug lug a log?**

◯ **Can a hog jig in the fog?**

◯ **Can a dog dig in the fog?**

◯ **Can Peg fit in a pot?**

◯ **Can Peg tug at a rug?**

PURPOSES OF THIS PAGE
1. to promote automatic word recognition within sentences that are questions
2. to promote sentence comprehension and interpretation
3. to give practice in detecting absurdities
4. to encourage creative and imaginative responses for discussion

27

It is Meg's pet.

2

It can nap in a hut.

It can dig a big pit.

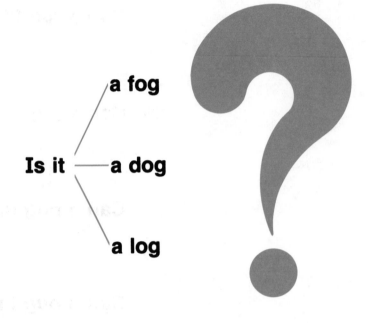

Is it — a fog / a dog / a log

It is tin.

It can tip.

It can get hot and wet.

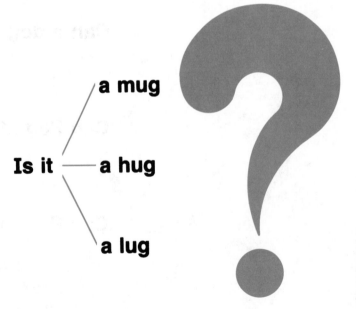

Is it — a mug / a hug / a lug

28

PURPOSES OF THIS PAGE
1. to promote automatic word recognition within sentences
2. to contrast phrases containing words of similar spelling or configuration
3. to promote sentence and paragraph comprehension
4. to give practice in reasoning logically and drawing conclusions

Is it in the fog?

○ **a cab**

○ **a dog**

○ **a rug**

○ **Meg**

○ **a hat**

○ **a van**

○ **a log**

○ **the ruts**

○ **Peg**

○ **a hog**

PURPOSES OF THIS PAGE
1. to promote automatic word recognition within phrases
2. to promote phrase comprehension through picture associations
3. to give practice in picture interpretation

29

2

It is a big, big mat.

It fits in a hut.

Dot can tug at it.

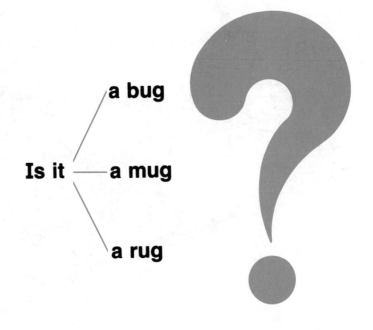

I can lug a big bag.

I can tug at a big rug.

I can hug lots of pets.

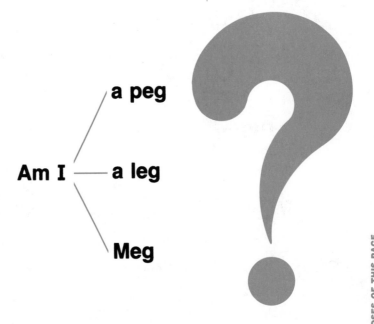

30

PURPOSES OF THIS PAGE
1. to promote automatic word recognition within sentences
2. to contrast phrases containing words of similar spelling or configuration
3. to promote sentence and paragraph comprehension
4. to give practice in reasoning logically and drawing conclusions

_ a _	_ i _	_ e _	_ o _	_ u _
	bin	Ben		bun
Dan		den	Don	
fan	fin			fun
				gun
		hen		
		Ken		
man		men		
pan	pin	pen		
ran				run
				sun
tan	tin	ten		
an	in		on	

SECTION 3 LETTER-SOUND CONTENT (pp. 31–46)
Review: Consonant letters
Review: Medial vowel letters *a, i, e, o, u*
New: CVC spelling pattern —*n (hen)*

31

3

□ hen

□ den

□ pen

□ men

□ ten

1

2

3

4

5

PURPOSES OF THIS PAGE
1. to promote automatic word recognition
2. to promote word comprehension through picture associations

PURPOSES OF THIS PAGE
1. to promote automatic word recognition
2. to promote word comprehension through picture associations

☐ **sun**

☐ **bun**

☐ **Ben**

☐ **run**

☐ **rug**

3

3

him

hen

ham

mat

Meg

men

pan

pen

pin

ban

bin

bun

Dan

den

Don

run

rut

rug

PURPOSES OF THIS PAGE
1. to promote automatic word recognition
2. to contrast words of similar spelling or configuration
3. to promote word comprehension through picture associations

○ **Meg's bun**

○ **Meg's bug**

○ **Ben's pen**

○ **Ben's pet**

○ **Dot's nut**

○ **Dad's net**

○ **Dad's mug**

○ **Sam's rug**

○ **Dan's pen**

○ **Dad's den**

○ **a hen's hut**

○ **a hen's pan**

PURPOSES OF THIS PAGE
1. to promote automatic word recognition within phrases
2. to contrast phrases containing words of similar spelling or configuration
3. to promote phrase comprehension through picture associations

3

○ Ben's hens run into the pen.

○ Ben lets the hen sit by the pan.

○ Don has ten big buns.

○ Don has ten tin men.

○ Pam has fun in the hen's pen.

○ Pam met a lot of pigs.

○ Ben gets a pen in Dad's den.

○ Ben sits on a cot in the den.

PURPOSES OF THIS PAGE
1. to promote automatic word recognition within sentences
2. to promote sentence comprehension through picture associations

1

2

3

4

3

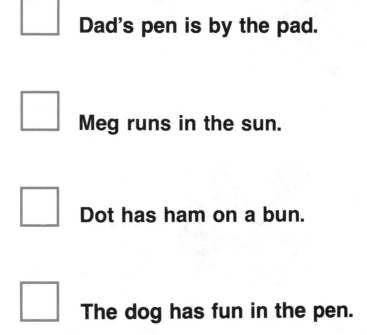

☐ Dad's pen is by the pad.

☐ Meg runs in the sun.

☐ Dot has ham on a bun.

☐ The dog has fun in the pen.

PURPOSES OF THIS PAGE
1. to promote automatic word recognition within sentences
2. to reinforce sentence comprehension through picture associations
3. to give practice in picture interpretation

The fat hen runs in the —

sun.

bun.

fun.

Dad sits on it in his —

pen.

hen.

den.

It is fun to jog and —

run.

rut.

rug.

Dot has a pal. It is —

Peg.

a pet.

a pot.

3

PURPOSES OF THIS PAGE
1. to promote automatic word recognition within sentences
2. to contrast words of similar spelling or configuration
3. to promote sentence comprehension through picture associations

○ "It's fun to run in the sun," said the hen.

○ "It's lots of fun in the sun," said Meg.

3

○ "Is the pen in the den?" said Dad.

○ "Is the pin in the bun?" said Dan.

○ Don said, "Rags sits in his pen."

○ Dad said, "Run and get the hens, Ben."

○ Don said, "The men can lug the rug."

○ Don said, "The men had lots of legs."

PURPOSES OF THIS PAGE
1. to promote automatic word recognition within sentences
2. to give practice in reading sentences containing quotations
3. to promote sentence comprehension through picture associations

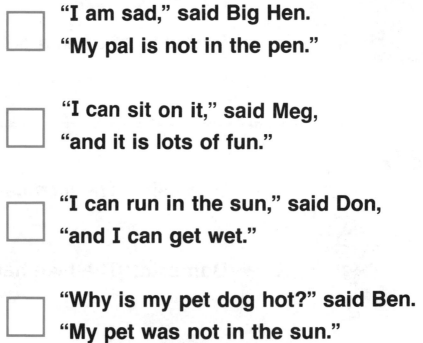

☐ "I am sad," said Big Hen.
"My pal is not in the pen."

☐ "I can sit on it," said Meg,
"and it is lots of fun."

☐ "I can run in the sun," said Don,
"and I can get wet."

☐ "Why is my pet dog hot?" said Ben.
"My pet was not in the sun."

PURPOSES OF THIS PAGE
1. to promote automatic word recognition within sentences
2. to give practice in reading sentences containing quotations
3. to promote sentence comprehension through picture associations
4. to give practice in picture interpretation

If Ken gets wet, let him sit in the — sit.

sun.

set.

If Dot digs in the sun, it is — fun.

fog.

fan.

If the dog sits on a log, it can — big.

beg.

bug.

PURPOSES OF THIS PAGE
1. to promote automatic word recognition within sentences
2. to contrast words of similar spelling or configuration
3. to promote sentence comprehension through picture associations

If a pet is hot, let it nap on a — met.

mat.

mug.

Can it?

○ Can ham fit on a bun?

○ Can a hen fit in a den?

○ Can a hen run in a pen?

○ Can a sun set in a den?

○ Can a bun run in the sun?

○ Can ten men get in a jet?

○ Can ten men sit on a pin?

○ Can ten hens get on a cot?

PURPOSES OF THIS PAGE
1. to promote automatic word recognition within sentences that are questions
2. to promote sentence comprehension and interpretation
3. to give practice in detecting absurdities
4. to encourage creative and imaginative responses for discussion

Is it in the pigpen?

○ Don in a hat

○ a hog in a pit

○ a pet in a bag

○ nuts in a jug

○ a hen by Don

○ a bug on a log

○ a pig at a pan

○ a log in a pen

○ Don in the sun

○ men in a cab

PURPOSES OF THIS PAGE
1. to promote automatic word recognition within phrases
2. to promote phrase comprehension through picture associations
3. to give practice in picture interpretation

43

It is big and hot.

Men sit in it and get tan.

It sets, but it cannot sit.

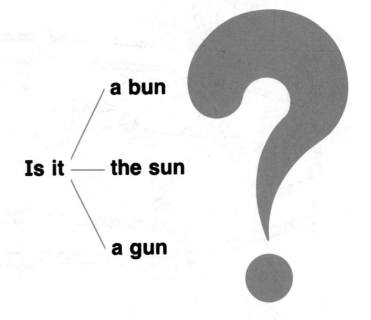

3

a bun

Is it —— the sun

a gun

Don is my pal.

I am not his pet.

I am not yet a man.

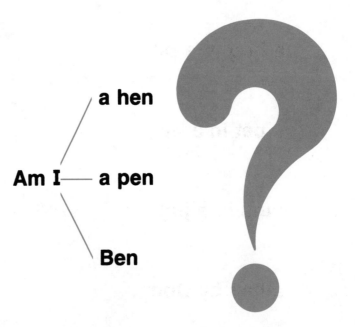

a hen

Am I —— a pen

Ben

PURPOSES OF THIS PAGE
1. to promote automatic word recognition within sentences
2. to contrast phrases containing words of similar spelling or configuration
3. to promote sentence and paragraph comprehension
4. to give practice in reasoning logically and drawing conclusions

Is it in the sun?

○ The hen sits in the sun and hits the pots.

○ The hen runs to get the fat bugs.

○ Don sits on a big log in the sun.

○ A pet sits on the log.

○ Don has a big, big hat.

○ Pam sits in the sun and has a lot of pots.

○ Pam sits in the sun and sits on a hen.

PURPOSES OF THIS PAGE
1. to promote automatic word recognition within sentences
2. to promote sentence comprehension through picture associations
3. to give practice in picture interpretation

It can run and dig in the sun.

It can get a lot of bugs.

It has a lot of fun in its pen.

3

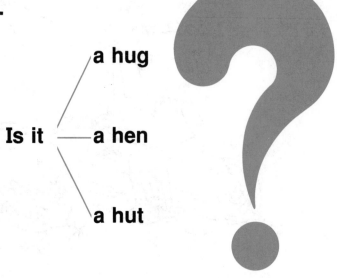

Is it — a hug

Is it — a hen

Is it — a hut

I had ten tin men.

I had a cap.

My dog Rags is my pal.

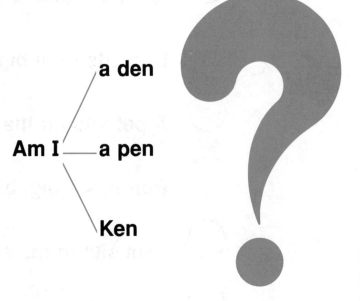

Am I — a den

Am I — a pen

Am I — Ken

PURPOSES OF THIS PAGE
1. to promote automatic word recognition within sentences
2. to contrast phrases containing words of similar spelling or configuration
3. to promote sentence and paragraph comprehension
4. to give practice in reasoning logically and drawing conclusions

_a_	_i_	_e_	_o_	_u_
bad	bid	bed		bud
		fed		
lad	lid	led		
mad				mud
		Ned	nod	
pad			pod	
	rid	red	rod	
		Ted		
cap				cup
	hip		hop	
map			mop	
		pep	pop	pup
tap	tip		top	
				up

4

SECTION 4 LETTER-SOUND CONTENT (pp. 47-62)
Review: Consonant letters
Medial vowel letters *a, i, e, o, u*
New: CVC spelling patterns—*d (bed)*
—*p (cup)*

47

☐ **bed**

4

☐ **bud**

☐ **mud**

☐ **mad**

☐ **Ned**

48

PURPOSES OF THIS PAGE
1. to promote automatic word recognition
2. to promote word comprehension through picture associations

PURPOSES OF THIS PAGE
1. to promote automatic word recognition
2. to promote word comprehension through picture associations

☐ **cup**

☐ **pup**

☐ **pop**

☐ **mop**

☐ **top**

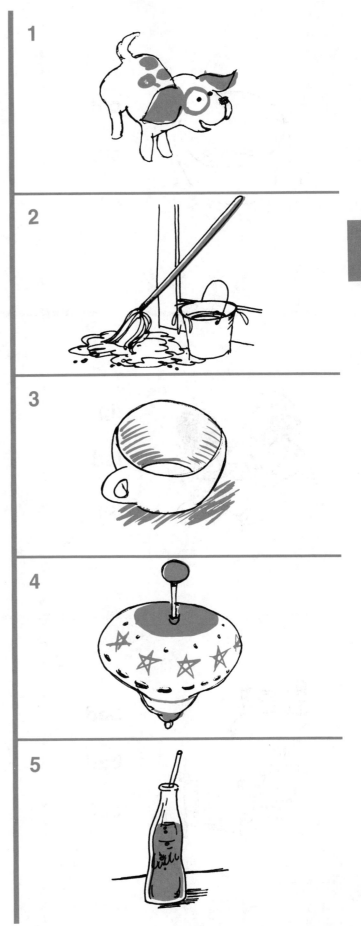

4

cot
cup
cap

top
tap
tot

fig
fed
fog

nod
Ned
Nan

bed
bad
but

pup
pop
pep

4

PURPOSES OF THIS PAGE
1. to promote automatic word recognition
2. to contrast words of similar spelling or configuration
3. to promote word comprehension through picture associations

○ **a hen's hop**

○ **Ken's top**

○ **a fat pup**

○ **a big cup**

4

○ **a wet mop**

○ **a red mat**

○ **a fat bud**

○ **a big bed**

○ **Nan's rod**

○ **a man's nod**

○ **a hen's hop**

○ **a pen's top**

PURPOSES OF THIS PAGE
1. to promote automatic word recognition within phrases
2. to contrast phrases containing words of similar spelling or configuration
3. to promote phrase comprehension through picture associations

◯ Ted fed his pup.

◯ Ted let his pup sit by him.

4

◯ The bug hops on its legs.

◯ The bug hops on the rod.

◯ The mad hen hid by a log.

◯ The log has a bud on it.

◯ The pup got mud on its legs.

◯ The pup ran on a rug.

PURPOSES OF THIS PAGE
1. to promote automatic word recognition within sentences
2. to promote sentence comprehension through picture associations

1

2

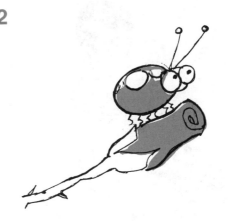

3

4

☐ The cup is by the pot.

☐ The mop is by the bed.

☐ The bug is on the bud.

☐ The pup is on a rug.

PURPOSES OF THIS PAGE
1. to promote automatic word recognition within sentences
2. to reinforce sentence comprehension through picture associations
3. to give practice in picture interpretation

Ted has to mop up the —— mad.

—— mud.

—— dam.

4

The pup got on top of the —— beg.

—— bed.

—— bud.

Ten men are in a —— pet.

—— jet.

—— wet.

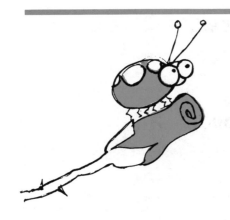

The red bug sits on top of a —— bad.

—— bid.

—— bud.

PURPOSES OF THIS PAGE
1. to promote automatic word recognition within sentences
2. to contrast words of similar spelling or configuration
3. to promote sentence comprehension through picture associations

○ Ned said, "The mop is on the big bed."

○ Ted said, "The pup is on my bed."

○ Kim said, "Why is the bud in the cup?"

○ Kim said, "Why is the pup in the mud?"

○ "I am not red yet," said the bud.

○ "I am not fed yet," said the pup.

○ "The dog is on top of the bed," said Meg.

○ "My log is on top of the bud," said Meg.

PURPOSES OF THIS PAGE
1. to promote automatic word recognition within sentences
2. to give practice in reading sentences containing quotations
3. to promote sentence comprehension through picture associations

4

1

2

3

4

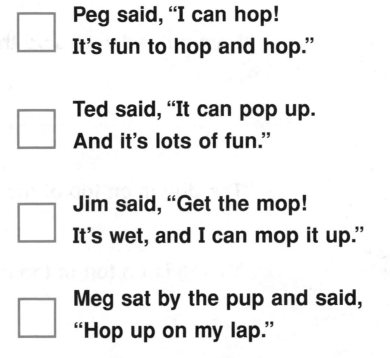

Peg said, "I can hop!
It's fun to hop and hop."

Ted said, "It can pop up.
And it's lots of fun."

Jim said, "Get the mop!
It's wet, and I can mop it up."

Meg sat by the pup and said,
"Hop up on my lap."

56

PURPOSES OF THIS PAGE
1. to promote automatic word recognition within sentences
2. to give practice in reading sentences containing quotations
3. to promote sentence comprehension through picture associations
4. to give practice in picture interpretation

If Ned gets mud on the mat, get him a

pop.

mop.

map.

If a pup is fed, it gets a lot of

pet.

pen.

pep.

If a man sits and nods, get him a

bed.

bad.

bid.

The bug is on the

fog.

dog.

log.

PURPOSES OF THIS PAGE
1. to promote automatic word recognition within sentences
2. to contrast words of similar spelling or configuration
3. to promote sentence comprehension through picture associations

Can it?

○ Can a pup hop in the mud?

○ Can a nod hop on a pod?

○ Can a mop get rid of mud?

○ Can a big bug hop on a red bud?

○ Can a pup sip pop in a cup?

○ Can a red hen hop in a bed?

○ Can Ted get fed in a bed?

○ Can Ned nod and nap in a bed?

4

PURPOSES OF THIS PAGE
1. to promote automatic word recognition within sentences that are questions
2. to promote sentence comprehension and interpretation
3. to give practice in detecting absurdities
4. to encourage creative and imaginative responses for discussion

Is it in the mud?

○ a fat pup   ○ sad Peg

○ wet Ned   ○ a bud

○ a red top   ○ a big bed

○ a big cup   ○ wet Meg

○ mad Ted   ○ a wet mop

PURPOSES OF THIS PAGE
1. to promote automatic word recognition within phrases
2. to promote phrase comprehension through picture associations
3. to give practice in picture interpretation

It is big and fat.

It can jig in lots of mud.

It runs and digs in a pen.

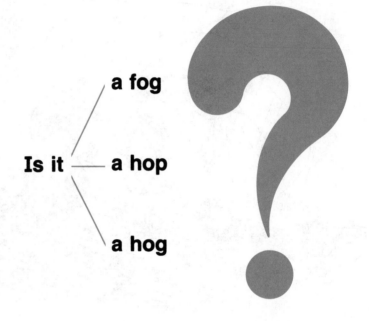

Is it
— **a fog**
— **a hop**
— **a hog**

It is Meg's pet.

It is a pal.

It gets up on Meg's bed to nap.

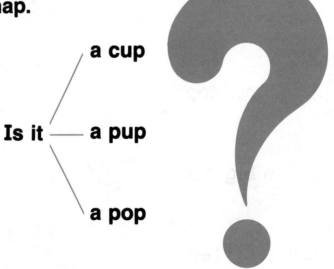

Is it
— **a cup**
— **a pup**
— **a pop**

PURPOSES OF THIS PAGE
1. to promote automatic word recognition within sentences
2. to contrast phrases containing words of similar spelling or configuration
3. to promote sentence and paragraph comprehension
4. to give practice in reasoning logically and drawing conclusions

Is it in the Big Top?

○ A dog sits by a man.

○ The dog has a red hat.

○ Ned has a can of pop.

○ A big red hen sits on a pup.

○ A man has lots of pups.

○ The man has a mop.

○ Ten men sit in the mud.

PURPOSES OF THIS PAGE
1. to promote automatic word recognition within sentences
2. to promote sentence comprehension through picture associations
3. to give practice in picture interpretation

61

It is Meg's.

It is red.

It cannot hop, but it's lots of fun.

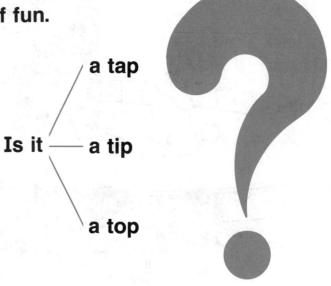

Is it — a tap

Is it — a tip

a top

It is wet.

A hog can hop in it.

A man can mop it up.

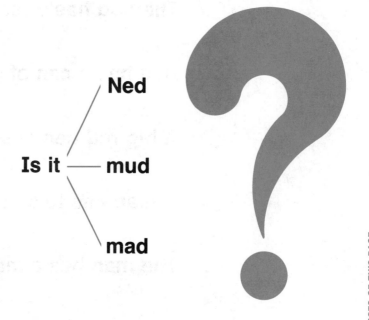

Is it — Ned

Is it — mud

mad

PURPOSES OF THIS PAGE
1. to promote automatic word recognition within sentences
2. to contrast words and phrases of similar spelling or configuration
3. to promote sentence and paragraph comprehension
4. to give practice in reasoning logically and drawing conclusions

_a_	_i_	_e_	_o_	_u_
				bus
gas				Gus
				us
		yes		
				gum
ham	him	hem		hum
			mom	
Sam				sum
tam	Tim		Tom	
	bib		Bob	
cab			cob	cub
jab			job	
	rib		rob	rub
			sob	
tab				tub
		web		

SECTION 5 LETTER-SOUND CONTENT (pp. 63–78)
Review: Consonant letters
Medial vowel letters a, i, e, o, u
New: CVC spelling patterns—s (bus)
—m (hem)
—b (rob)

5

☐ web

5 ☐ cob

☐ cub

☐ Bob

☐ bus

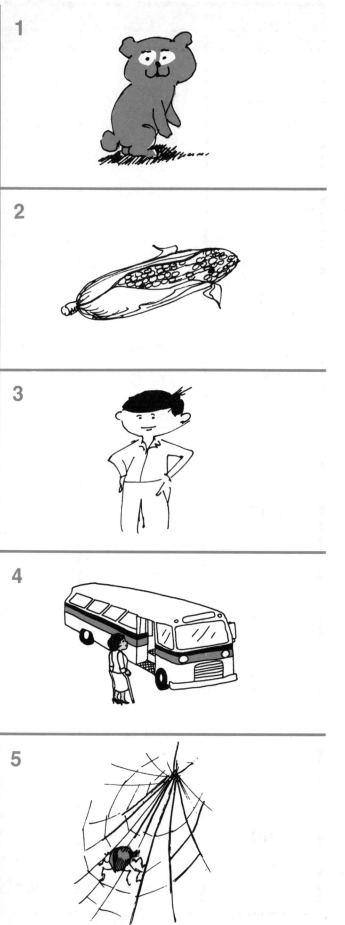

PURPOSES OF THIS PAGE
1. to promote automatic word recognition
2. to promote word comprehension through picture associations

PURPOSES OF THIS PAGE
1. to promote automatic word recognition
2. to promote word comprehension through picture associations

☐ **Mom**

☐ **Tom**

☐ **gum**

☐ **gas**

☐ **hum**

5

mop

Mom

men

gas

gum

got

tug

tub

tab

cob

cub

cap

hum

hem

him

bud

bus

Bob

PURPOSES OF THIS PAGE
1. to promote automatic word recognition
2. to contrast words of similar spelling or configuration
3. to promote word comprehension through picture associations

○ Mom hems.

○ Tom hums.

○ A pup digs.

○ A cup dips.

○ A bug runs.

○ A pup rubs.

○ A pet hugs.

○ A bug hums.

PURPOSES OF THIS PAGE
1. to promote automatic word recognition within sentences
2. to contrast sentences containing words of similar spelling or configuration
3. to promote sentence comprehension through picture associations

○ A rug rips.

○ A man mops.

○ A hen hops.

○ A cat hems.

○ The bus gets gas.

○ The bug is on Sis.

○ Tom hugs a cub.

○ Tim runs a cab.

○ Mom fed the ham to Wag.

○ Bob said, "I can hum."

○ Tom has a pet cub.

○ Mom has a tin tub.

PURPOSES OF THIS PAGE
1. to promote automatic word recognition within sentences
2. to promote sentence comprehension through picture associations

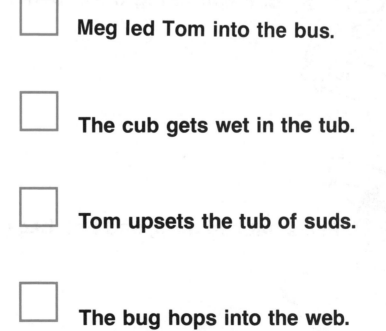

☐ Meg led Tom into the bus.

☐ The cub gets wet in the tub.

☐ Tom upsets the tub of suds.

☐ The bug hops into the web.

PURPOSES OF THIS PAGE
1. to promote automatic word recognition within sentences
2. to reinforce sentence comprehension through picture associations
3. to give practice in picture interpretation

Val's job is to run a ———
- cob.
- cab.
- cup.

Kim did not get on the ———
- bus.
- bug.
- bud.

5

Bob had to tug the cub into the ———
- ten.
- top.
- tub.

Peg's hat had a rip, and Peg began to ———
- rob.
- sob.
- hum.

70

PURPOSES OF THIS PAGE
1. to promote automatic word recognition within sentences
2. to contrast words of similar spelling or configuration
3. to promote sentence comprehension through picture associations

○ Min has ten hens and a cub.

○ Ron had a job on the bus.

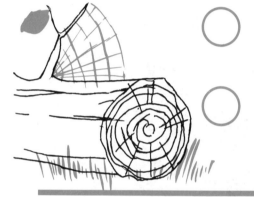

○ The log has a cobweb on it.

○ The tub has a bobcat in it.

5

○ The bug began to rub mud on its leg.

○ The pup sits up in the mud to beg.

○ The bug hums and hops.

○ The dog sits and sobs.

PURPOSES OF THIS PAGE
1. to promote automatic word recognition within sentences
2. to promote sentence comprehension through picture associations

71

1

2

5

3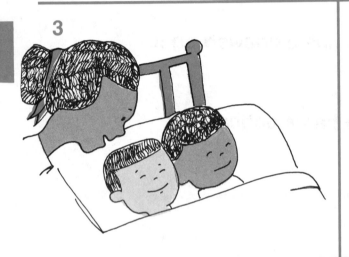

4

☐ "If my pup sits in my lap," said Dot,
"I can pet it and hug it."

☐ Tom is in bed and so is Ben.
"Why not hum a bit?" said Mom.

☐ Sam said, "It's fun to sit in the sun.
But my job is to run a bus."

☐ "Let's go on a bus," said Liz.
"Ten of us cannot fit in a cab."

PURPOSES OF THIS PAGE
1. to promote automatic word recognition within sentences
2. to give practice in reading sentences containing quotations
3. to promote sentence comprehension through picture associations
4. to give practice in picture interpretation

Liz can pin up the
- hum.
- him.
- hem.

Liz ran to get the
- cob.
- cub.
- cab.

5

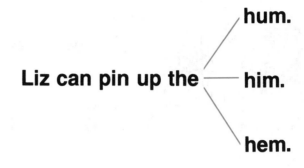

Meg got rid of the
- bus.
- buds.
- bugs.

Tom's job is to rub the
- cub.
- tub.
- mud.

PURPOSES OF THIS PAGE
1. to promote automatic word recognition within sentences
2. to contrast words of similar spelling or configuration
3. to promote sentence comprehension through picture associations

○ Ron said, "Get on the bus, Wag."

○ Don said, "Sit on the bug, Bud."

○ "The sunset is so red," said Roz.

○ "A bug's in the cobweb," said Mom.

○ "The cob is on the top," said Meg.

○ "The cub is in the tub," said Peg.

○ Dot and Ted said, "Run to us, Wag."

○ Mom and Ned said, "Run to the bus, Wag."

PURPOSES OF THIS PAGE
1. to promote automatic word recognition within sentences
2. to give practice in reading sentences containing quotations
3. to promote sentence comprehension through picture associations

5

Can it?

○ Can a wet cub run on gas?

○ Can a fat bug hum by a red bud?

○ Can a fat cub jab a big rib?

○ Can a tan cab jab a big bus?

○ Can a red bib fit in a tin tub?

○ Can a tan bug hum and sit in a web?

○ Can a red bug sit and hem a bib?

○ Can Tom's mom rub a wet bus?

5

PURPOSES OF THIS PAGE
1. to promote automatic word recognition within sentences that are questions
2. to promote sentence comprehension and interpretation
3. to give practice in detecting absurdities
4. to encourage creative and imaginative responses for discussion

Dot can sit in it.

Dot gets wet in it.

Mom rubs suds on Dot in it.

5

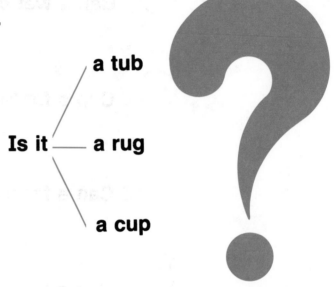

Is it
- a tub
- a rug
- a cup

It can get on Sis.

It can hum and hum.

It can get into a web.

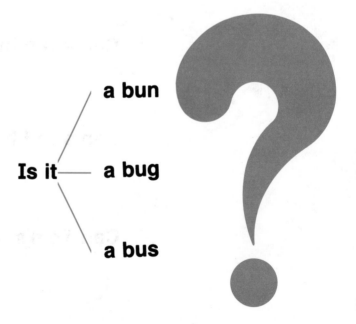

Is it
- a bun
- a bug
- a bus

PURPOSES OF THIS PAGE
1. to promote automatic word recognition within sentences
2. to contrast phrases containing words of similar spelling or configuration
3. to promote sentence and paragraph comprehension
4. to give practice in reasoning logically and drawing conclusions

Is it on the rug?

PURPOSES OF THIS PAGE
1. to promote automatic word recognition within phrases and sentences
2. to promote phrase and sentence comprehension through picture associations
3. to give practice in picture interpretation

5.

○ a cub in the tub

○ suds in the tub

○ Tom in a hat

○ Tim's job is to sob.

○ Tom's job is to rub a cub.

○ a red bug in a web

○ a red cab in the fog

○ suds on the red rug

○ a big cup of suds

○ Tom hums to the cub.

77

It can go "pop!"

It is lots of fun.

Tom had it and said, "Yum, yum."

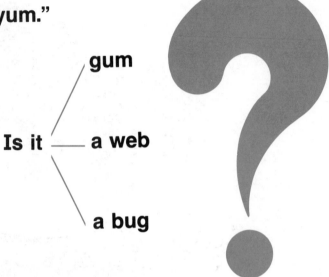

Is it —— gum / a web / a bug

5

It runs on gas.

A lot of men can get in it.

Roz and Dot can sit in it.

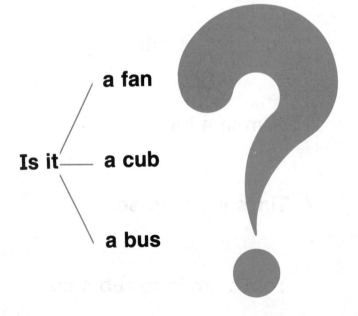

Is it —— a fan / a cub / a bus

PURPOSES OF THIS PAGE
1. to promote automatic word recognition within sentences
2. to contrast phrases containing words of similar spelling or configuration
3. to promote sentence and paragraph comprehension
4. to give practice in reasoning logically and drawing conclusions

_a_	_i_	_e_	_o_	_u_
			box	
	fix		fox	
Max	mix			
	six			
wax				
ax			ox	

SECTION 6 LETTER-SOUND CONTENT (pp. 79–94)
Review: Consonant letters
Medial vowels *a, i, e, o, u*
New: CVC spelling pattern —x (*wax*)

6

□ **ax**

□ **ox**

6

□ **fox**

□ **box**

□ **sob**

80

1

2

3

4

5

PURPOSES OF THIS PAGE
1. to promote automatic word recognition
2. to promote word comprehension through picture associations

☐ **six**

☐ **fix**

☐ **mix**

☐ **Max**

☐ **wax**

1

2

3

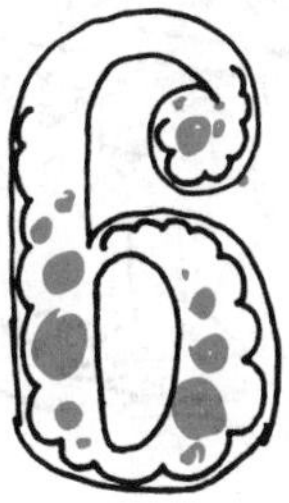

4

5

6

PURPOSES OF THIS PAGE
1. to promote automatic word recognition
2. to promote word comprehension through picture associations

○ a red box

○ a big fox

○ a box of mix

○ a can of wax

○ a wet mix

○ a wet Max

○ the hot wax

○ a fat fox

○ a big ax

○ a big ox

○ Mom and Max

○ Mom and mix

PURPOSES OF THIS PAGE
1. to promote automatic word recognition within phrases
2. to contrast phrases containing words of similar spelling or configuration
3. to promote phrase comprehension through picture associations

○ **Max and the fox**
○ **mix in a box**

○ **an ax in a log**
○ **an ox on a leg**

○ **six and ten**
○ **six cans of tin**

○ **box in a pen**
○ **fox in a den**

○ **tag on a box**
○ **tap on a fox**

○ **six cups by Sis**
○ **six caps by Max**

PURPOSES OF THIS PAGE
1. to promote automatic word recognition within phrases
2. to contrast phrases containing words of similar spelling or configuration
3. to promote phrase comprehension through picture associations

6

○ A red rox runs into his den.

○ A cub is in the big box.

6

○ Six men led the big ox into a pen.

○ Six bugs ran into the cobweb.

○ Tom can wax the jug.

○ Tom can mix the jam.

○ Roz is six and gets a hat.

○ Roz can fix up the ten men.

PURPOSES OF THIS PAGE
1. to promote automatic word recognition within sentences
2. to promote sentence comprehension through picture associations

PURPOSES OF THIS PAGE
1. to promote automatic word recognition within sentences
2. to reinforce sentence comprehension through picture associations
3. to give practice in picture interpretation

☐ Meg's job is to fix the bed.

☐ Jim's job is to rub the jugs and mugs.

☐ Dot's job is to fix the box.

☐ Tom's job is to rub the cub.

6

The ox can jig on a
- bat.
- box.
- fox.

Mom can fix Jim's
- box.
- wax.
- bus.

Tom can hug a
- cap.
- cab.
- cub.

Pam fed the six
- dogs.
- hogs.
- hens.

6

PURPOSES OF THIS PAGE
1. to promote automatic word recognition within sentences
2. to contrast words of similar spelling or configuration
3. to promote sentence comprehension through picture associations

○ "I can get the fox," said Max.

○ "I can fix the box," said Max.

○ "I can wax it," said Max.

○ "I am six," said Max.

6

○ "Yes, I can fix it," said Mom.

○ "No, I cannot mix it," said Mom.

○ Dad said, "The ax is in the box."

○ Dad said, "The wax is in the can."

PURPOSES OF THIS PAGE
1. to promote automatic word recognition within sentences
2. to give practice in reading sentences containing quotations
3. to promote sentence comprehension through picture associations

1

2

6

3

4

☐ "If the fox cannot fit in the box," said Max, "let it run in the pen."

☐ Dad said, "If Don gets my ax, I can cut the logs."

☐ Tom said, "I can mix the jam if Max can get the pan."

☐ "The wax is hot," said Mom, "but I can get it."

PURPOSES OF THIS PAGE
1. to promote automatic word recognition within sentences
2. to give practice in reading sentences containing quotations
3. to promote sentence comprehension through picture associations
4. to give practice in picture interpretation

Dot's job is to fix a
- box.
- fox.
- ox.

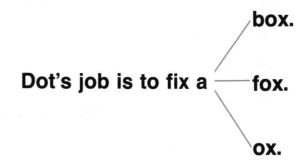

Sam's job is to run a big
- bug.
- box.
- bus.

6

Wag zips by on the
- web.
- wet.
- wax.

The fan is by the
- fix.
- fox.
- fit.

1. to promote automatic word recognition within sentences
2. to contrast words of similar spelling or configuration
3. to promote sentence comprehension through picture associations

Can it?

○ Can a red fox sit in a den?

○ Can Max's ax fit in a box?

○ Can six cubs mix the wax?

○ Can six cobs fix the top?

○ Can a tan ox lug a big box?

○ Can Mom's pet fox wax a bus?

○ Can Max rub and wax six jugs?

○ Can a fox rub suds on an ox in a tub?

6

PURPOSES OF THIS PAGE
1. to promote automatic word recognition within sentences that are questions
2. to promote sentence comprehension and interpretation
3. to give practice in detecting absurdities
4. to encourage creative and imaginative responses for discussion

Is it in the fox's den?

6

○ **a fat hen**

○ **a red fox**

○ **a big pot**

○ **a big ox**

○ **a can of wax**

○ **a red box**

○ **a box of mix**

○ **six hot mugs**

○ **six big logs**

○ **a red ax**

PURPOSES OF THIS PAGE
1. to promote automatic word recognition within phrases
2. to promote phrase comprehension through picture associations
3. to give practice in picture interpretation

It can sit in a den.

It can run in the sun.

It can hop on a log.

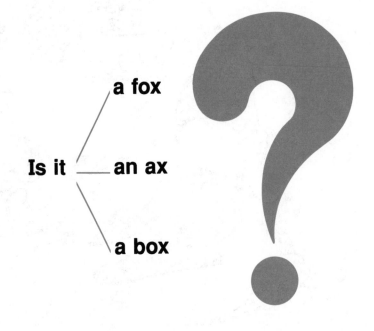

Is it — a fox / an ax / a box ?

6

It is big.

It can tug a big tub.

It can lug a big log.

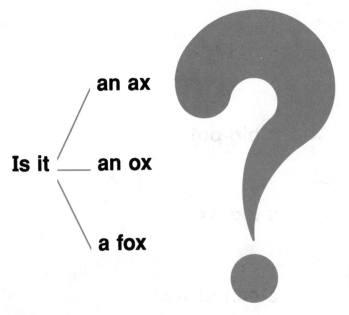

Is it — an ax / an ox / a fox ?

PURPOSES OF THIS PAGE
1. to promote automatic word recognition within sentences
2. to contrast phrases containing words of similar spelling or configuration
3. to promote sentence and paragraph comprehension
4. to give practice in reasoning logically and drawing conclusions

Is it in the Big Top?

6

	Yes	No
A man is in a net.	⊗	○
A man is at the top.	○	○
A fox sits on a box.	○	○
A cub is on a tub.	○	○
The ax is in a log.	○	○
A can has wax in it.	○	○
A hat has lots of dots on it.	○	○

1. to promote automatic word recognition within sentences
2. to promote sentence comprehension through picture associations
3. to give practice in picture interpretation

I am red.

My bed is in a den.

I am as big as a dog.

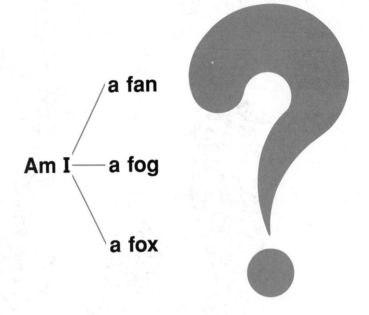

a fan

Am I —— a fog

a fox

6

I got a big red box.

The box had a pet in it.

I am big and I am six.

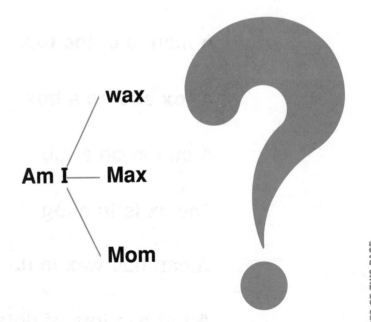

wax

Am I —— Max

Mom

PURPOSES OF THIS PAGE
1. to promote automatic word recognition within sentences
2. to contrast words and phrases of similar spelling or configuration
3. to promote sentence and paragraph comprehension